# THE JOURNEY TO HEALING & RESTORATION

6 Tips To Support Your Spouse In Recovery From a Porn Addiction

# ANGEL WILLIAMS

FOREWORD BY TITANYA JOHNSON

# Praise Reports

"This book can help anyone who is supporting someone with any type of addiction. Replace the word porn with food, drugs, alcohol, anything."
— Christina Espinoza Kempthorne

"Angel Williams provides an honest perspective on how porn addiction has affected her marriage through the years. With this book, Ms. Williams brings addiction from the shadows into the light, taking readers through her journey of betrayal and pain. Ms. Williams shows us that through love, compassion, and their faith in God, she and her husband continue to find ways to re-establish their commitment to their marriage and love for each other. A significant amount of shame surrounds the challenges of addiction; only through honesty and openness can healing begin. This vulnerable account is a must read for those who feel lost and alone in their own struggles within their marriage."
— Zoe Reyes, LMFT

# Praise Reports
## continued

"In The Journey To Healing & Restoration, Angel Williams offers admirable integrity and compassion as she shares her vulnerable journey with vicarious and harmful addiction. Exploration of the many internal battles that tested her faith are told with empathy, humility, and transparency as a woman of God. This book speaks to individuals who deal with the juxtaposition of acknowledging one's own emotional needs while supporting and existing in the shadows of a partner's struggle with addiction. Spiritual verses offer comforting passages as coping tools that guide readers in a relevant manner. Ms. Williams has captured an easy to relate to experience of trusting God through relational challenges that tests one's self-love in the face of wavering faith and uncertainty. This book is a testimony of faith and the love that binds partners to the other side of addiction."

– Carnetta Porter, PsyD

**6 TIPS TO SUPPORT YOUR SPOUSE IN RECOVERY FROM A PORN ADDICTION**

# THE JOURNEY TO HEALING & RESTORATION

ANGEL WILLIAMS

FOREWORD BY TITANYA JOHNSON

Copyright © 2021 by Angel Williams

All rights reserved. No part of this book may be reproduced or transmitted in any form or by any means, electronic or mechanical, including photocopying and recording, or any information storage and retrieval system, other than "fair use" as brief quotations embodied in articles and reviews, without prior written permission from the publisher.

All scripture quotations are from the American Standard Version marked as (ASV).

ISBN 978-1-7371131-0-2

Printed in the United States of America

# Dedication

This book is dedicated to

# LOVE

# Special Thanks

First, I would like to thank my dear husband, Ernest, for encouraging me to write this book so that others may be encouraged. His unwavering commitment to personal development and health is inspiring. The Almighty knew what He was doing when He brought us together. Thank you for loving me unconditionally.

I would also like to express my deepest gratitude to my Mother and Father for their love and support. Thank you for teaching me how to love unconditionally.

A special thanks to my cousin, Sonia. She's been "my person" since our youth. I appreciate her wise advice and unbiased opinion on absolutely everything! I know that I can always count on her to be listening ear. She is my trusted confidant. I love you, cousin.

I would also like to thank the T.O.T writers and The Greats group members. Thank you for your friendship, the sharpening, and most importantly, your prayers. I love you all and look forward to reading each of your books.

# Special Thanks
## continued

One last shout out to my dear friend and coach, Titanya Johnson (Lady Ty The Great). Thank you for your obedience to the Holy Spirit and for sharing knowledge. Thank you for pushing me to dig deep and tap into "greatness". None of this would be possible without your obedience to God. You are a leader in every sense. I love you, Ty.

# CONTENTS

- Foreword
- Introduction
- Tip 1: Transparency..........................................13
- Tip 2: Forgiveness & Grace.........................21
- Tip 3: Seek Help.................................................24
- Tip 4: Setting Boundaries.........................30
- Tip 5: Healing & Restoration....................33
- Tip 6: The Most Powerful Resource....36

# Foreword
BY TITANYA JOHNSON

It has been my pleasure to know the author Angel for many years. Angel has been such a delight to know as a human first, as a supporter of my book, Daddy Issues, and a student in a discipleship course. I had the pleasure of facilitating a Master Life discipleship group of dedicated individuals for 24 weeks. Angel was dedicated and committed throughout the entire course, super supportive of every classmate. She went from student to disciple to teacher to mentoring and discipling others. Angel is a master builder. Angel's willingness to want to be an amazing human strives for a complete understanding of how to love like God. I have watched her grow in her relationship with God. Throughout the many years that I have known Angel, she has been an encourager, motivator, and full of joy. Angel is a friend not only to me but a friend of God.

Angel recently took a step in the direction of becoming an author by attending the T.O.T. Triumph Over Trauma writers course. This six-week course teaches 1st-time authors how to self-publish their book. The dedicated person she is, her book was complete before the class was over. I'm beyond impressed with Angel's consistency and execution in all she does. The message Angel has to deliver is a message of deliverance. Many will be set free after reading this book.

I'm excited for the world to meet Angel, the author. She is courageous and bold. Ask me why I say that? Angel is a private person, but in this book, she opens up and shares life experiences and testifies so that others may be healed and set free. The heart Angel has is huge. She wrote this book not for herself but for others going through challenging times. The topic of this book is shocking to many. Why? Because we often hide from struggles, never getting healed. Authentic and real in every measure, Angel will not let you be trapped. She has written a book filled with so much light and love that you will have victory and be set free. Rev 12:11 says, "They overcame by the blood of the lamb and the word of their testimony." Thank you, Angel, for being triumphant and testifying that others may overcome.

This book you are about to read is transparent truth, and Angel offers understanding and support, and tools to unlock anyone who has dealt with this. Angel's character is honest and obedient. Therefore I am excited to support and read every book Angel writes. She wrote this book with an anointing that will break yokes. Angel is a loving wife, disciple, friend, and author. I am blessed to share one of God's gifts to me, Angel the Author. Nickname Earth Angel!

By Titanya Johnson,
"Lady Ty The Great"

# Introduction

Addiction is not only challenging for those in recovery, but it also impacts those that support them too. In this book, I share my personal experience supporting my husband in his recovery from porn addiction, including tips and resources that we are using to heal ourselves and our marriage. I believe that recovery, healing, and restoration are possible based on my experience. I am not a certified counselor, and I am not engaged to provide psychological or any other type of professional advice. I am sharing my experience, hoping that it helps others feel less alone and inspires readers to get the help they may need.

Some of the experiences I share may trigger you to think of your own experiences. I encourage you to give yourself the grace and time needed to work through your thoughts and feelings. I found that journaling my experience and writing this book has helped in my healing process. Journaling is a beneficial self-care technique that reduces stress. It can also bring clarity to thoughts and feelings, help gain control of emotions, and improve mental health. The healing process takes time, so be kind to yourself and your spouse. You are worth it, your spouse is worth it, and your marriage is too. Healing is possible.

# TIP 1
# **Transparency**
## Bringing it all to the light
―――――⊙―――――

Transparency is the key that unlocked the door to my husband's recovery journey, our healing process, and newfound intimacy. Because of my husband's transparency, I can share my experience. In the past, exposing my vulnerabilities, fears, desires, and perspective regarding my husband's porn use was not easy for me to share with him or others. However, I have since learned that there are many benefits of being transparent, so I choose to be open about our experience to inspire others to do the same.

Truth be told, before accepting Jesus into my life and marrying my husband, I did not look at porn negatively. I was neutral when it came to pornography and watched it a few times myself. However, after asking God into my heart, I started to read the Bible and my beliefs on many things changed.

"Ye have heard that it was said, Thou shalt not commit adultery: but I say unto you, that every one that looketh on a woman to lust after her hath committed adultery with her already in his heart." (Matthew 5:27-28, ASV)

Pornography causes the viewer to look upon women or men lustfully, and when he or she has done this, the viewer has committed adultery. Therefore, pornography is adultery. Before learning this, I thought adultery was committed through physical touch or an emotional affair. Boy, was I wrong! The sobering truth is that infidelity and addictions are just a couple of a long list of reasons that many couples get a divorce.

Let's face it you probably feel even more betrayed after learning that porn is adultery. I have been there too, and it's valid for you to feel grief-stricken and betrayed. It takes time to process our feelings when we find out about our spouse's betrayal and addiction. It's essential to take time to think about whether ending the marriage or trying to save it is the best choice for both of you. Although many studies share that infidelity and addictions are among the top reasons for divorce, it does not have to be the end to your love story. Most issues can be resolved if both parties are open to working on them. I chose to stay in my marriage because we both decided to do the work required to recover and heal. We hope that our story provides you with some encouragement along your journey. Recovery and healing are possible. However, if you are in an abusive or emergency situation, I encourage you to seek help immediately.

Before sharing information about the resources we have utilized, it's essential to share the early stages of our journey. In 2004 I asked God into my heart and had settled in my mind that I would serve God. Six months after this commitment, I went on my first missionary trip to Uganda, Africa. During the trip, I was offered a job at an orphanage in Uganda. Upon returning home, I prayed and fasted for clarity on making the right decision. Two weeks later, I decided to decline. The same evening I decided while at church, my husband introduced himself to me the same evening. Looking back, I see that God had different plans for me. My husband and I courted for two years, intending to get married. It was such a sweet courtship filled with prayer, dates in the park, bible studies, serving in ministry together, lengthy conversations about our dreams and future, and meeting each other's families. I must share that this relationship was unexpected and everything I never thought was possible. After a two-year courtship, we married then moved in together. Living together was a massive change for us both. We were two months into our marriage when I first found out about my husband's porn use. During that time, I was more hurt because I felt deceived because this was out of his character. It made me question everything about him. All kinds of negative thoughts flooded my mind because I felt betrayed.

This discovery also surfaced some old insecurities regarding trust. I had a deep-rooted fear of abandonment and not being wanted because my biological father was never consistent in my life. At that time, I was not mature enough to see past my pain or deal with my baggage. I never told anyone about this early experience because I was ashamed. Just two months prior, our friends and family celebrated our union at our wedding reception held at our church. I also thought that if I shared what happened, they would judge him, and I did not want people to think differently of us. I was too prideful to ask for help and didn't know I needed help for myself. I also felt responsible for those that God put in my circle of influence and did not want to let anyone down. So, I fasted and prayed. I knew that God would not stop the work he started in either of us, and I trust God, so I held on tightly to those promises.

During the discovery, my husband apologized, so I said that I forgave him. He immediately took steps to cut off anything that would tempt him to watch porn. He threw out his computer, canceled the cable, and was also very selective about what he watched when watching movies. I was not too fond of that part because I enjoyed watching movies, but I sacrificed to show my support. He also sought counsel from a trusted elder at our church.

We did everything we thought was suitable for Christian newlyweds. Time passed, and although things "looked" okay on the outside, I kept my insecurities to myself for years. I never shared this with my husband because I did not want my husband to view me as weak. I also wanted to protect my husband's reputation, so I never sought counsel for myself. As time passed, we spent more time doing busy ministry activities, and we never dealt with any of our issues. My pain came out in how I would communicate with my husband or respond to his touch. There was a lack of intimacy because I was still hurting from the betrayal and did not realize I was also carrying unforgiveness in my heart. I thought I had forgiven him, but because we never dealt with the root causes of our issues, it continued to impact our marriage. After a year of serving, we made a tough decision to take a step back from ministry to work on our marriage. We spent more time together, sought professional council, took some steps to heal our marriage. We attended self-improvement seminars, marriage seminars and applied what we learned. Life went on.

Years passed, and I would have this nagging feeling that he never stopped watching porn, but I gave it to God to handle. Sometimes he would share that he had watched it, and he would apologize. I would say I forgave him (i.e., swept it under the rug), then we'd move on. I would ask myself, who was I to point the finger when I had sins of my own. Occasionally thoughts would enter my mind, and I would tell myself at least he is not physically cheating on me; this was my way of coping and rationalizing it. Although it was not the healthiest thing to do for our marriage, I did it to keep the peace because everything else in our life was great. Also, I'm not too fond of confrontation or anything that brings division, so much that I was willing to deceive myself, not knowing that I was robbing us both of the possibility to have a healthy, thriving marriage. I fooled myself for years by sweeping things under the rug.

Fast forward fifteen years later, and the battle with porn is not yet over. After asking my husband about charges on our bank account that I thought were fraudulent charges, my husband shared that he needed help because he has a problem with porn. He also shared that he was seeking professional help from a counselor. During this time, I was already aware that my husband was going through something, so I would pray for him and knew that he would talk to me in time.

When he did share, he expressed remorse. It was hard to see the pain and shame on his face when he shared his truth. However, regardless of how painful it was to hear the raw truth, his transparency set us both free. The day he chose to be transparent about his reality, the chains of unforgiveness broke, and a heavyweight lifted from my shoulders. Because my husband was vulnerable enough to share his truth, this started us both on our pathway to healing and recovery. The wall that was once around my heart came down. I now know that being transparent about your truth is vital to begin the healing process. Because of my husband's transparency, I can speak freely about my truth now. God is so faithful, and this is another answered prayer.

# Notes

# TIP 2
# Forgiveness & Grace

"and be ye kind one to another, tenderhearted, forgiving each other, even as God also in Christ forgave you." (Ephesians 4:32, ASV)

The day my husband decided to be transparent about his truth, the wall fell from around my heart, and I finally forgave him. I am so grateful for his transparency.

Through this experience, God has also allowed me to see my husband how He sees him. Oh, what a beautiful sight it is to look upon someone as God sees them. Because of this, I can extend the same grace and forgiveness to my husband that God extends to us all. I know that my husband will overcome this addiction and triumph over his past traumas. God will finish the work he started in us both. He can do the same for you and your spouse too. If God raised the dead and gave eyesight to the blind, I am confident in His abilities to heal you, your spouse, and your marriage.

> God will finish the work he started.

God is in the business of making us whole; nothing missing, nothing broken. I believe this wholeheartedly because of God's faithfulness in answering my prayers; my faith has increased over the years. I am now rooted and grounded in my faith. I know who I am and what my God-given purpose is. Knowing these things can only be obtained by spending time with God in prayer, learning who God is through hearing and reading His word. As long as I stay connected to the vine (God), I can walk in the fruit of the Spirit, which is love, joy, peace, patience, kindness, goodness, faithfulness, gentleness, and self-control. Walking in the fruit of the Spirit allows me to bear ALL things in LOVE. It gives me the ability to forgive my husband if/when relapses occur without putting a wall back up. It also gives me the ability to walk by faith and not by sight.

You have access to all of this too. Therefore, I encourage you to do a study on forgiveness and grace. Also, ask God to guide you through this journey.

# Notes

# TIP 3
## Seek Help

Seeking counsel for help is not a sign of weakness. On the contrary, many Bible verses tell us that wise people seek counsel, and those who don't are fools and fall.

> "Where no wise guidance is, the people falleth;
> But in the multitude of counselors there is safety."
> (Proverbs 11:14, ASV).

> "Whoso loveth correction loveth knowledge;
> But he that hateth reproof is brutish."
> (Proverbs 12:1, ASV)

Based on scripture, I encourage you to seek counsel from someone specializing in addiction and marriage counseling. Join a support group and or an online community. You can also confide in a trusted friend. Remember, scripture says a "multitude of counselors." I find it encouraging to know that God knew we would face situations that require guidance and help from others and that He has already equipped counselors with the wisdom and understanding to help those in need. Based on my personal experience, wise counsel and support are needed for this battle. It's also crucial for you to seek counsel to begin your healing process. You can be a positive influence in your spouse's recovery process. Healing is possible for you both.

You may be feeling like your spouse's porn watching was your fault. You may have had the following thoughts, I am not pretty enough, I am not skinny enough, or maybe you have compared yourself to the actors in porn videos, Etc. All of those thoughts are lies. Repeat after me, **my spouse's porn addiction is not my fault.** It took me fifteen years of marriage to fully understand this. While researching, I learned that most porn addictions pre-date marriages. For example, my husband was introduced to pornography at a very young age by mistake. A relative had left a movie on in their bedroom and fell asleep. My husband had walked in and saw it playing. This happened a couple of times as a child. He also experienced some traumatic things as a child and later developed a habit of watching porn to deal with his unresolved feelings of what happened to him. As an adult, interactions with the person that hurt him as a child would trigger the use of porn to self-medicate to cope with negative emotions. Working with a counselor to understand the root causes that triggered the use of porn was a huge breakthrough. Empowered with this knowledge, my husband can respond to negative emotions more healthily now. Recovery is a process, and it takes time to discover, recover, and heal. So if you plan to stay in the marriage, be prepared for the battle. Every situation is different. It's not a one size fits all solution.

I am thankful to God because my husband took the initiative to seek counsel for himself without any prompting from me. This made it easier for me to support him in the recovery process. However, it's not all roses and blue skies. Although God told me to "love him through it," I still have moments of weakness where feelings of betrayal creep up when relapses occur, but I have learned to cancel out the negative thoughts and believe the best. I continue to stay focused on God's promises. I must share, if you decide to support your spouse in their recovery journey, there is a possibility that he/she may relapse. I pray your spouse does not relapse; however, it does happen, and per professionals, it is normal.

The first few times my husband relapsed, it was challenging for me. Each time is like a sucker punch to the gut that brings moments of confusion and heartache. However, I remember reading in the Bible that confusion is not of God, so I've quickly reminded myself of that, which helps me a ton. Although the heartache is real and valid, I promise healing is possible.

Our communication has gotten better, and my husband is transparent about his struggles and relapses. By him communicating, it has taken the secrecy out of the equation, and it's changing the old habit of watching porn and creating a new way for him to deal with his emotions. We now understand how and why the habit was formed, why he watches it, and what triggers him to watch it. Seeking counsel was the best decision my husband could have made for himself and our marriage. It has also allowed us to rebuild trust and intimacy. Our journey is not over, but we are heading in an excellent direction.

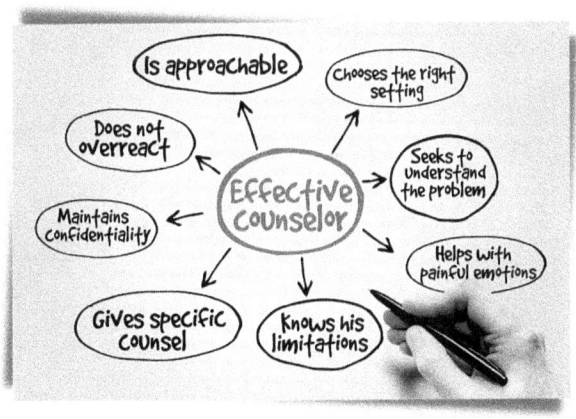

Having shared this small part of our journey, I encourage you to educate yourself on what porn does to the brain and learn the steps needed to break a porn habit. Habits develop over time, and breaking them is no easy task. It will all take time and work.

I found many free resources on the Covenant Eyes website at www.covenanteyes.com. One helpful resource I found on the site is, *The Porn Circuit, Understand Your Brain and Break Porn Habits In 90 Days,* written by Sam Black. The information provided in this book has helped me so much. Educating myself has equipped me with a better understanding of supporting my husband. There are so many other great resources on this site too. I encourage you to browse the site.

# Notes

# TIP 4
# Setting Boundaries

Setting boundaries is beneficial on the road to recovery. When my husband first came to me and shared his truth and plan to seek counsel, I was led by the Holy Spirit to hold my tongue, extend grace and give him the time needed to seek counsel. Setting up boundaries for myself was no easy task. I had to reframe from taking my husband's daily temperature, even though it was at the forefront of my mind. We women generally like to know every detail. Thanks to the Holy Spirit, I had an understanding that asking him daily if he had a relapse would not be beneficial to his recovery. I believe it would only make him think I thought less of him and didn't trust him. And that is the furthest from the truth. I am inspired by my husband's willingness to be courageous enough to own his truth, and I am super proud of him for taking steps to deal with past traumas. So, setting boundaries for myself has been very rewarding, although not easy at times. My husband now has a safe place to heal, and I am thankful to God for that.

In addition to setting boundaries for myself, my husband also set up boundaries. When he first told me about his truth, he threw out his laptop.

He also set up an account through Covenant Eyes to report porn use on his phone to an accountability partner. He reached out to a trusted friend who overcame a porn addiction to be his accountability partner. This step showed me that he was serious about his recovery and willing to try everything possible for recovery. I must also share that he only utilized this service for a short time. At first, I was sad to hear that he canceled the subscription. However, after he explained why he canceled the subscription, it made sense. He shared that he did not want to put a temporary band-aid on the issue because he desires to get the root of why and fix the problem to be porn-free. He has since discovered the root cause of why and what triggers him, so progress is being made.

I share this part of our journey because not every technique or resource may help. Part of this journey is learning about different resources and applying the best methods for your specific situation. There is not a one size fits all solution. Each case and the circumstances are unique to each individual. What may work for some may not work for others. So again, give your spouse and yourself the grace and time needed to find what works best for their recovery, but whatever you do, don't give up. There are plenty of resources out there. I will share with you the most powerful resource in the last chapter.

# Notes

# TIP 5
# Healing & Restoration

Now on to the good stuff! Healing and restoration are possible! My marriage is living proof; so much has already been accomplished. Although we've not made it to the final destination just yet, we are heading there, one victory at a time, and learning to celebrate each victory along the way. Writing this book and removing my mask is a huge victory for me. I am facing all the fears that I once had of being judged and sharing my truth. I hope that my transparency helps others to do the same. I no longer have to live in bondage. The shackles of keeping this secret have fallen off, and I can now look in the mirror as a free woman and embrace my authentic self. I am living my God-given purpose to help set the captives free by testifying how God can take a broken, cracked vessel and make it whole, filing in each crack with something better and more substantial that will reflect the work of the master potter, God. Nothing missing, nothing broken. He can do the same for you and your spouse.

**Celebrate each victory!**

I must also share that it's important to celebrate and recognize the small victories along the way. We can often be so focused on the final result that we miss out on the small accomplishments. It's also important to reward yourselves for doing the work too (e.g., dinner date, a couples massage, a weekend for two at the beach, etc.). Also, find other reasons to celebrate each other and embrace the newfound intimacy produced during this journey. The work can be heavy at times, but the rewards of a healthy, thriving marriage far outweigh the sacrifices made to get there.

# Notes

# TIP 6
# The Most Powerful Resource

The most powerful resource that I have relied on during this journey is God's word. His words have been a lamp unto my feet, guiding me every step of the way. His words have encouraged me, given me the strength to endure, and the understanding and wisdom to be the best helpmate and support to my husband. None of this would be possible without God. As you embark upon your journey of healing and supporting your spouse in their recovery, I encourage you to implement the following daily foundational practices:

1. Spend time reading God's word. If you are unsure of where to start, do an internet search with the following keywords:
- What does the Bible say about who God is
- What does the Bible say about me
- What does the Bible say about love
- What does the Bible say about forgiveness
- What is the fruit of the spirit
- What does the Bible say about marriage/divorce
- What does the Bible say about healing
- God's promises for my life
- What does the Bible say about prayer and fasting

2. Meditate on God's promises.

3. Pray: This is your personal phone line to God.

4. Fast: People in the bible generally fasted when they believed for something to change or needed clarity on something.

5. Put on the whole armor of God (read Ephesians 6:10-18)

The road to recovery and healing is not quick, but the rewards of a healthy, thriving marriage are worth the time it takes. If you don't see change quickly, please don't lose hope. God hears your cries for help. He has not forgotten about you. Please continue to cast all of your concerns at His feet, and allow Him time to complete the work he started in you and your spouse—nothing missing, nothing broken. Allow the master potter time to mold the broken vessels. You are his masterpiece.

Lastly, this is a spiritual battle, so be prepared to fight with your sword, God's truth. Put on the whole armor of God daily and be prepared for those fiery darts. With God, all things are possible. Through prayer, fasting, counseling, and unconditional love, you and your spouse will be victorious!

"And Jesus looking upon them said to them, With men this is impossible; but with God all things are possible."
(Matthew 19:26, ASV)

"For I know the thoughts that I think toward you, saith Jehovah, thoughts of peace, and not of evil, to give you hope in your latter end. And ye shall call upon me, and ye shall go and pray unto me, and I will hearken unto you."
(Jeremiah 29:11-12, ASV)

> With God, all things are possible.

# Notes

# Notes

# Important

The information provided in this book should not be substituted for professional or medical advice and should not be used to diagnose, treat, or develop a treatment plan. The author's intent is only to offer information of a general nature to help encourage and inspire readers. If you use any of the information in this book, the author and the publisher shall not be liable for any physical, emotional, financial, or commercial damages, including, but not limited to, special, incidental, consequential, or any other damages. If you are in a life-threatening or abusive situation, please seek professional help immediately.

For other life-enriching books, bulk orders, or to book an author interview please visit: https://skyangelpublishing.company.site/

www.ingramcontent.com/pod-product-compliance
Lightning Source LLC
Chambersburg PA
CBHW070942160426
43193CB00011B/1786